99

THOUGHTS

ON HEARING GOD'S CALL

LEARNING TO
LISTEN AND RESPOND
TO GOD'S VOICE

JOHNNY SCOTT

99 Thoughts on Hearing God's Call
Learning to Listen and Respond to God's Voice
Copyright © 2011 Johnny Scott

Visit our website: **simplyyouthministry.com**

Credits
Author: Johnny Scott
Executive Developer: Nadim Najm
Chief Creative Officer: Joani Schultz
Editor: Janis Sampson
Cover Art Director: Riley Hall
Designer: Riley Hall
Production Manager: DeAnne Lear

ISBN 978-0-7644-6527-7

10 9 8 7 6 5 4 3 2   20 19 18 17 16 15 14 13 12

Printed in the United States of America.

CONTENTS

INTRODUCTION

Esther was an orphan who became a princess...that's when the *real* adventure started. Even though she lived in a grand palace, Esther had her own set of very real problems. She had to figure out how to navigate her own treacherous surroundings in the king's court while the lives of the Jewish people—*her* people—were being threatened. Esther won the approval of the king and through a dramatic sequence of events was put in a place by God to save a nation.

While you're not navigating the perils of palace life, the teenage years can certainly be a dangerous landscape that seems to take no prisoners! Like Esther, you have the same desire: You want to know God's calling for your life. Esther figured out that everything in her life had happened perfectly, so she'd be in the right place at the right time and could save God's chosen people from destruction. God used Esther in a powerful way. What an exciting life she lived for him! I'm sure she was scared and she didn't always know what to do. Do you ever feel the same way? Ever wonder what God is calling you to do? You know the risks, and so did she.

Hearing God's call on your life is the start of the greatest adventure of all! This isn't kid stuff. The stakes are high. A lot of people on the planet are in some way trying to hear God's call. While there are no plans that work the same for everyone, this book will show you some steps that others have used. Maybe you picked up this book and the truth is you feel guilty because you don't really know how to even *want* to hear God's call. Perhaps you're afraid and you know you should be listening to God in so many moments in your life, but starting to do it has seemed difficult. The good news is that like many other things, with practice, you can grow in this area. There is a *huge* promise you should know as you start to read this book. This promise is from God himself, and it can be found in James 4:8; it says, *"Come close to God, and God will come close to you."*

Johnny Scott

FIRST THINGS FIRST

Thoughts 1 to 11

These first few thoughts are all about getting your feet wet. You can jump around, read ahead, or plow straight through! All of the thoughts in this book are about hearing God's calling on your life. If the whole idea of hearing God's voice is a new idea to you, then you are not alone. Many people don't think God has anything to say to them, but he does, and as you will learn he speaks in some far-out ways. If you are wrestling with believing that God would want to talk to you, then honesty is a great place to start. Before you begin to read this book, tell him exactly what you're thinking; he already knows anyway, so revealing your true feelings will clear the air so you can start fresh. God is big enough to take on all of our honesty.

Which one of the following places best describes what you currently feel about hearing God's calling (or hearing God at all) in your life?

- I feel like I hear God and know my specific calling.
- I feel like God is trying to tell me what he wants me to do, but I still don't understand him yet.
- I am afraid to hear God's call on my life.
- I don't think God has anything to say to just me.
- I think God only talks to some people.
- I think God only talks to me when I am good.
- God used to talk to me, but for some reason he doesn't anymore.
- I've never thought about God talking to me, but I'm excited to learn.

Whatever describes your thoughts about hearing God, you can be sure that this book will change them. You might want to always have a Bible handy while you're reading this book so you can see how many of these thoughts come straight from God's Word, the Bible.

01 Your past doesn't determine your future calling by God.

Where you come from has nothing to do with how, where, when, or why you are called. We are all used to being judged by others. It seems like people want to decide for us at times what we can accomplish based on what they see. God doesn't work that way.

What's different about God's calling is that *"people judge by out-ward appearance, but the Lord looks at the heart" (1 Samuel 16:7).*

Satan wants to keep you from hearing God's call.

+ EXTRA THOUGHT

Read Psalm 51 (and especially verse 17!).

Satan will tell us we don't deserve to experience God because of things we've done wrong. But that's when we need to be with God more than ever! God will not turn you away when you're broken before him. Don't let Satan steal moments with God from you!

It's never too late to hear God's call.

When we grow away from God, it usually happens so slowly that we don't notice our moments with him slipping away. While it may take awhile to slip away, it only takes one decision on our part to re-engage in a moment spent with God. That's great news for all of us. God runs to us when we take the first tiny step. Read the story in the Bible from Luke 15:11-32 about a father and a son. The father in the story represents God. It shows exactly how God is patiently waiting for us to take one step back toward him.

You hear more when you listen with your whole heart.

Things get in the way of hearing God when you make them more important than God. The Bible calls anything put above God idolatry. One quick way to do a checkup on this is by looking at how you spend your time, money, and energy. If there is something competing for the number one spot in your heart, you have to cut it out of your life. Jesus says that we can't have two masters or we will love one and hate the other (Matthew 6:24).

Hearing (and obeying) God's call is serious business!

Following God's call on your life should have warning labels all over it that read: DANGEROUS!!! USE EXTREME CAUTION. It's rarely the easiest, most comfortable choice. When you realize that there's no other choice but to follow God, that's when things get very exciting. You will see...keep on reading!

Warning! Warning! Don't use God's calling as an excuse.

Using God's calling as an excuse can be dangerous. God's hope for our lives is a very personal and serious matter. It should never be used by us to get us out of things we don't want to do. I had a friend who was dumped by a girl. She told him, "God is not calling me to date you." While this may be true in some cases, my buddy not only got dumped by the girl, but he felt like he got dumped by God! Bummer.

07 You're not on your own!

It's so important to God that you hear his calling on your life that he sent a Helper just to make sure you hear him. This Helper is called the Holy Spirit, and he comes to live inside of us when we ask Jesus to be the Lord of our lives.

+ EXTRA THOUGHT

The Holy Spirit can even talk in a language only God understands that tells God what we're thinking and feeling. Even when we can't put our thoughts into words, God understands us. Romans 8:26 says, *"And the Holy Spirit helps us in our weakness. For example, we don't know what God wants us to pray for. But the Holy Spirit prays for us with groanings that cannot be expressed in words."*

Before you ever wanted to hear God's calling, he was pursuing *you*!

Are there moments from your past when you felt really close to God? Go back to those experiences, and thank him for being with you then. Think through some of your best and most difficult memories. Think of how God was working even if you didn't see it then.

 Are you afraid of hearing God's true calling for your life?

Think about this: You should be more afraid of not following God than of anything other people can do to you. Proverbs 29:25 says, *"Fearing people is a dangerous trap, but trusting the Lord means safety."*

Sometimes people don't hear God's call because they have shut him out of areas in their lives.

Have you done this with certain things you don't want him to have control over? Think of everywhere you go and what you do. Where do you feel the farthest from God? Go through this exercise: Speak out loud and invite God into everything you do in a normal day, even the goofy stuff.

If you want to know God's plan for your life, just *ask*!

God listens when we pray. There is power in simply asking God for his plan. It's not only the easy way out, but it's smart! Sometimes he wants to teach us valuable lessons through our journey. He is a God of action—he doesn't want to see us struggle unnecessarily to find his will for our lives.

HEAR WHAT GOD CALLS EVERYONE TO DO

Thoughts 12 to 20

God's call to everyone is a great place to start because we are not left in the dark when it comes to hearing God's voice and will for our lives. He wants us to clearly know how to serve him. Not only does God have an awesome plan made just for your life, but he also has a launching pad that every follower of Jesus starts on. Hearing God's personal calling on your life will be an epic story with crazy twists and turns. Here are some general thoughts you can count on being true!

+ EXTRA THOUGHT

God has general things he calls everyone to. This is a great place to start to find out what he called *just you* to.

How do I know for sure that God has a calling just for me? Check out Ephesians 4:11-13: *"It was he who gave some to be apostles, some to be prophets, some to be evangelists, and some to be pastors and teachers, to prepare God's people for works of service, so that the body of Christ may be built up until we all reach unity in the faith and in the knowledge of the Son of God and become mature, attaining to the whole measure of the fullness of Christ." (NIV)*

You are called by God to community.

God uses a picture of the human body to describe what the church is like and how we all fit into it (see Romans 12:4-8). Some people are hands and others are feet, but every part is important and serves the others in a unique way. When you are not serving the whole church, you are not functioning the way God intended, and everybody misses out.

- Get to know others at your church—attend a prayer meeting and join a small group or Sunday school class.
- Find a place to serve at church—join the greeting team, help out in the nursery, or help with lawn care.

- Engage in the collective journey your church is on. What is God calling your church to do in the community?

You are called by God to love God.

God gave Moses the Ten Commandments after he called the people of Israel out of Egypt. At the beginning of our great history as God's people, the first things he called us to do could all be summed up in one simple statement: Love God (Exodus 20:1-7).

You are called to love people.

Loving people is not something that God gifts only parts of the body. We are all called to love others. This is so important to God that he made half of the Ten Commandments all about how we should love other people (Exodus 20:8-17).

Jesus summed up all of the Ten Commandments into one thought in Mark 12:30-31: " *'And you must love the Lord your God with all your heart, all your soul, all your mind, and all your strength.' The second is equally important: 'Love your neighbor as yourself.'* " Can you match each one of the Ten Commandments (Exodus 20:8-17) under loving God or loving people?

You are called by God to service.

Not everything in our calling is going to seem like a great adventure. There are things about every amazing calling that seem like hard work. One way to really freak people out is to do these things with joy as if working for the Lord and not for people (Colossians 3:23).

You are called by God to sacrifice.

Sacrifice might seem like a scary or even dreaded word, but God is calling everyone who follows him to sacrifice. This goes against what comes natural to us. In fact, we are constantly being told by messages all around us to stop sacrificing and treat ourselves.

One message can be seen in commercials to buy things that are centered only around our needs. We are slammed with cues everywhere that have the underlying message, "Be smart—do things this way because it will be easier on you."

It's not wrong to take care of our own needs. The problem is the starting point. When we follow the example of Jesus, our starting point is serving other people. Sacrifice starts when we see the needs of other people and make that a priority over ourselves. When you sign up to listen to God's call on your life, you're in for lots of twists and turns in the road. Here's a secret to life we learn from Jesus about sacrifice: We receive joy when we sacrifice. Read one of the most influential sermons Jesus ever preached to a crowd. It's found in Matthew chapter 5–7. He describes all kinds of ways to sacrifice and what the outcome will be if you do! Romans 12:1-2 talks about what it means to be a "living sacrifice" as our calling.

Not every person is going to be called to suffering; but bad things happen to good people all the time. No one expects everything to be peachy all the time, so when tough times come remember this: God seems to speak more clearly than ever during dark moments. When bad times hit, God will be there with you.

17   You are called by God to forgive.

Nobody ever said that hearing your calling from God would
be easy. Forgiveness isn't always easy but it is something we are
all called to do, and Jesus led by example. While we were still
sinners, Jesus forgave us (Romans 5:8)!

+ EXTRA THOUGHT

Feel like you're hitting a roadblock as you try to hear God's
voice in your life? Perhaps he has called you to take one
step before any others. Consider whether he is being silent
or if perhaps you haven't yet been obedient since he last
spoke. Forgiving others can be a wonderful experience
for those you forgive but mostly for your own heart. If
you want a breakthrough, consider doing a forgiveness
inventory. Are there people you need to forgive?

18   You are called by God to worship.

Worship isn't just for those artistic people. Everyone is called to
worship. If singing or painting for God isn't your thing, then do
whatever you do best as worship for God! Imagine how your next
soccer game could be your own personal worship service. It's all

about your starting point. Dedicate everyday things you are good at to God and enjoy them as worship to the Lord.

You are called by God to share who Jesus is.

Sharing Jesus isn't only for preachers. When God starts to change who you are from the inside out, the excitement should spill out of your life like a cup that is overflowing. Our natural human response is to talk with people about whatever is most important to us or first in our hearts. See one way the Bible explains it here: Luke 6:45.

You are called to be a priest!

Really? Before Jesus came, only priests were allowed to talk to God in holy places within the tabernacle. Because Jesus was obedient to his calling, we are the holy place where God lives. All Christians are actually greater than the old priest gig! Check this out: *"You are a chosen people. You are royal priests, a holy nation, God's very own possession. As a result, you can show others the goodness of God, for he called you out of the darkness into his wonderful light"* (1 Peter 2:9).

23 PRACTICAL THINGS GOD COULD BE CALLING YOU TO DO RIGHT NOW!

Thoughts 21 to 43

Don't make the mistake of overcomplicating hearing God's calling on your life. The best place for you to start might be going through this super easy list of things you can do right now!

21 Watch someone's kids for free!

Think of a person with kids who needs help, like a single parent or a pastor. Bring a board game with you, and clean up a little before the parent comes home. If you want to serve a person, loving his or her children is one of the most significant ways to show them!

22

"Adopt" a single mom, widow, or widower for one year...

...and invite them to spend special days and holidays with you and your family. While something like this may seem small to you, God can use it in a big way. Of course, make sure to talk with your mom or dad before extending the invitation.

23

Visit a nursing home.

Take a group of friends with you, and sing, play checkers, and pray with seniors. You will be the hands and feet of Jesus as you show love to those people.

24

Volunteer at a local community center, after-school program, or Boys & Girls Clubs.

Start with the little things that take only time and your willingness. Your openness to hearing God will grow and so will your ability to hear when he calls. Don't sit around waiting for the big call. Try serving in some small ways so you'll be in good practice when God calls on you for the next level!

Sit with kids at lunch who need friends.

Don't make this a big show. Be very private about it so you honor the person you are serving. Ask God to help you think of yourself as you ought to. As we love others we actually love Jesus. Keeping this verse in mind helps us not to think more highly of ourselves than the people we serve: " *I tell you the truth, whatever you did for one of the least of these brothers of mine, you did for me'* " *(Matthew 25:40 NIV).*

Thank a teacher, coach, parent, sibling, friend, or stranger.

A person's whole day can be brightened by two little words everybody knows and rarely anybody says—thank-you. You know how good it makes you feel when someone recognizes your efforts. When you do say thank you, it feels more sincere when you go out of your way to make the point so here are some thank-you hints: Think about if you should show your appreciation in front of other people or not. It may make them nervous or doubt your motivations. There is a time to recognize efforts publically and a time to be private. Pray about the perfect time and way to say thank-you.

Listen to people!

When you slow down and take the time to hear what people are saying, your eyes may be opened to a world of ways to bless others. Even if you can't help, the simple act of listening can change someone's life. Everyone wants to be heard.

Go in one day a week for two hours and help out your youth minister or someone else working at the church.

Send one encouraging personal message to a different one of your friends each day.

Ask your friends what you could pray for them about. Start a journal of your prayers. Send notes asking those friends for updates.

Coach a little league sports team (with an adult) for the purpose of loving people like Jesus did.

Get to know the kids on your team and pray for them.

Stay away from TV for 40 days.

Spend your spare time reading books that encourage you spiritually, or find ways to serve others, help out at home, and so on.

Tutor a younger kid in a subject or activity you know well.

It may be easy for you to understand and excel at a certain subject in school. That means that this is something you can bring to God for him to use. Never discount whatever abilities you may have. While it may seem like a small thing to you God can use it in big ways.

"Adopt" an elderly couple or elderly person and offer to maintain their yard or help with housework for a year.

Start a prayer group at your school.

Meet one time a week to pray for the school, the administration, the teachers, and the student body. Pray for God's kingdom to come to your school. Just pray!

Do random acts of kindness...

...without anybody else knowing anything about it.

 ## Start leading a weekly devotion with your family.

As a family, read some Scripture and make a list of things that you are praying for as a family together.

 ## Organize a toy drive from Thanksgiving to Christmas for some less fortunate kids in your community.

Deliver the toys by Christmas Eve.

 ## Initiate a weekend of nonstop prayer at your church.

Shoot for 24 or 48 hours of nonstop prayer! Set up a prayer room, and ask people to sign up for 30-minute time slots.

 ## Clean your room without being asked.

**Help with a VBS for a whole neighborhood of kids.**

**Save money so you can take a non-Christian friend to church camp or a youth group retreat.**

**Skip lunch one day a week at school and use that time to pray for your school.**

+ EXTRA THOUGHT

Visit claimyourcampus.com to see other ways you can find your calling at your school.

**Invite a friend to church.**

If all your friends already go to church, make some new friends who don't so that you can ask them. Get a new job or join a club where you don't know anybody. Do what it takes to put yourself in a place where you can meet new people who don't know Jesus.

TOP 10 THOUGHTS ON HEARING GOD'S CALL

Thoughts 44 to 53

Hearing God's call and reconnecting to him through his Son Jesus, is what the whole Bible is about. These 10 thoughts on hearing God's call are top ways the Bible says to plug in and listen, so start *here*!

 44 **Praying is one of the best ways to hear God's call.**

Even Jesus prayed to his Father in heaven about his calling. He also taught the disciples how to pray in Matthew 6:9-15 (read it!). Here are some tips on praying:

- Don't use big words to impress God. He's cool with you talking normal.
- Start by praising him for who he is.
- Thank him for the good things he has done.

- Be specific when you ask.
- Don't know what to pray? Pray Scripture. Find a psalm that you like, and pray that psalm for a week.

45 *Slow down* to hear God.

In the Old Testament this was done on the Sabbath. When we run constantly from one thing to the next, we don't make any room to be still and silent. Take a whole day to rest your mind. Do something out of the ordinary that brings joy to you. This can be different for every person. The point is to take your speed from 80 mph to a slow walk.

46 Write out your story of how you are listening to God's call.

Journaling can be a really fun and eye-opening tool for hearing God talk to you. This will give you the chance to read back and see all the things you have written in the past. You will be able to see how God was with you in good times and bad.

47 Getting away from the ordinary can help you tune in to God's voice.

Nobody likes to be uncomfortable. Whether it's in the food you eat, being around new people and new cultures, or just being out of your normal routine, God can use that experience to challenge you and help you tune in to what God is saying. Some people even force themselves into new situations just so they can rely more on God.

Want to experience more moments with God? Step out into something new. Take a journey, a quest, a trip...

48

Sing, dance, create!

One of the first things we learn in the Bible is that we are made in the image of God himself. One thing God does

+ EXTRA THOUGHT

The idea of getting away to plug into God is actually as old as dirt itself. A big word for this is *pilgrimage*. So create and go on your own modern-day pilgrimage. It doesn't have to be a huge ordeal; you can get away with God to listen to him even through a short walk.

well is creativity. Just look at the world around you! In fact, he started the whole Bible by telling the story of how he created the world. Taking time to be creative *for the purpose of listening to him* is a great way to hear God's call. So paint. Sculpt. Draw. Dance. Sing. Compose. Write. Let your creativity soar!

Make a big deal about creatively worshipping God!
Before you start your creative project, pray out loud
and ask God to be with you, speak to you, and connect
with you while you create.

49 Read God's Word.

It's going to be very difficult to hear God's calling on your life if
you don't really know who he is. When you read God's Word,
you're seeing all the things he's done in the past and hearing what
his will is for the future. Here are some tips on reading God's
Word:

- You can read the same small section everyday and ask
  God to help you understand it. This is called meditating.
  You keep the same Scripture on your mind for days at a
  time so you can get a deeper understanding.

- Skip around! You can find reading plans at
  youversion.com that will help you not get bogged down
  in one section.

- Did you know that if you read three chapters a day in
  the New Testament, you'll finish the whole thing in three
  months?

50   Fasting is like a rocket ship to hearing God's voice.

Fasting is denying yourself something to glorify God and go deeper with him in the Holy Spirit. This can be powerful because whenever we think about the thing we are giving up, our thoughts automatically focus back on why we are giving it up. Not only does fasting refocus us constantly, it also opens up huge blocks of time to spend in prayer, Bible reading, and other activities to help us hear God's voice. Consider fasting from TV, video games, or a make a special lunch date every week where you don't eat and instead spend that time with God.

51   Trek out on your own!

Some people are really good at spending "alone" time, but others of us have to take a friend when we go to the bathroom. It's not just girls either! All people think differently when they're alone. We think deeper because there are no distractions. The big word for this one is *solitude*. You may even need a whole day just to get your mind to slow down before your time of real solitude begins. Plan ahead: Get chores done, homework caught up, and Facebook notified. *Get off the grid!* Even get your family involved by letting them know you plan to be alone for a few days. No need to leave your neighborhood. Stay in your room, take walks, and practice serious solitude.

Hear God by encouraging others.

Encouraging others can be a surprisingly fun way to hear God's calling, but be careful—like a yawn in study hall, encouragement is very addicting!

Everyone is called to give generously.

God calls us all to live in a "backward" kingdom. It's true—Jesus said some things that seemed against the flow of common sense; but when you dig deeper you hear a calling that rings true. Try telling a little boy at Christmastime that it's better to give than to receive (Acts 20:35). He will look at you like you're *crazy*! *What's wrong with you?! Don't you like presents?* Of course, we all do; but when you have given generously, you start to hear the voice of God.

FAMOUS CALLS OF GOD TO HEROES IN THE BIBLE

Thoughts 54 to 64

We can learn how God might call us by looking at how he called others from the Bible. We learn about who God is, what he is like, and how he deals with us by looking at the Bible. God never changes. (He even says that about himself in Malachi 3:6, *"I am the Lord, and I do not change."*) The following thoughts are all centered on real people who were called by God in the Bible. Be sure to grab some time to read some of these true stories on your own.

 ### 54 Don't be surprised at how God calls you!

And don't assume he won't do it in some crazy way! Think of how he called these people:

- Mary—God sent an angel in the night (Luke 1:26-38)
- Baalam—God talked through a donkey
  (Numbers 22:1-35)
- Moses—God talked through a burning bush (Exodus 3)

God sent a prophet to anoint David with oil, but it was only after David had grown very close to God in many quiet moments and adventures (1 Samuel 16). God told Noah to build a boat in a desert (Genesis 6). *Crazy*! We need to keep our hearts and imaginations open. You serve a creative God, who can speak to you in ways only you would understand. This is one way he shows himself to us personally.

55 God may use friends to help you hear him...or just talk to you himself!

God called out to a young boy named Samuel (1 Samuel 3) in the middle of the night, but Samuel didn't get it at first. If you want to recognize the voice of God, it's good to hang out with people who know what his voice sounds like. This happened to Samuel. His teacher, Eli, helped him to figure out it was God calling him. If Eli hadn't helped Samuel he might have missed out.

+ EXTRA THOUGHT

Jesus is the perfect example when it came to being in the world but not of it—especially in his friendships! We see many examples of how Jesus loved and welcomed every person, no matter what their background was. We should follow his example in this way. We also see Jesus gather spiritually minded friends around him at critical moments in his life. When Jesus was faced with a tough decision or situation, he reached out to those friends who were of the same mind as he was.

+ EXTRA THOUGHT

Late at night is a great time to listen to God because all the distractions of the day are gone and you are usually in a quiet, peaceful place getting ready for bed. You can make this a time you purposefully quiet yourself and ask God to call out to you.

56 Sometimes God calls us and we refuse to listen.

In fact, some people in the Bible did just this, and God continued to pursue them in strange ways. Baalam's donkey talked to get his attention and Jonah was thrown overboard while trying to escape God. (Jonah's story gets a whole book in the Bible. Read it for yourself!) You might already know that Jonah ended up in the belly of a great fish. The point is, when God calls, he means business.

57 Obeying God's call is about faith.

Abraham is one of the first heroes in the Bible who shows us that being called by God is all about faith. Abraham didn't know anything about God when he was called to take his family and leave his home forever, but he did it anyway. It is just as hard to obey God's call today as it was in Bible times! Read the famous faith chapter that talks about Abraham and others in Hebrews 11.

58 God doesn't want you to be confused about your calling.

God is not a God of confusion but of peace (1 Corinthians 14:33). He doesn't want you to be unsure of his calling for your life. In fact, he wants to be sure we know, so he tries in many ways to let us know his will. Gideon was called by God to save the people of Israel (Judges 6) and since that's a big job you wouldn't want to be wrong about, he asked God in some weird ways to assure him of his calling. God does just what Gideon needed—he made his will crystal clear.

+ EXTRA THOUGHT

Faith is described in Hebrews 11:1 as "the confidence that what we hope for will actually happen; it gives us assurance about things we cannot see." When we wrestle with trying to find out what God is calling us to do, we may come to a point in which we have to step out on what we feel even when it looks crazy. Following God is an adventure like none other.

59 God calls people that others never would!

David had seven older brothers who were all bigger, stronger and each thought to be the chosen one the prophet Samuel was looking for. David's own father didn't even believe he was being called by God! But in fact, David was called by God even when other people didn't see why (1 Samuel 16).

You don't have to be afraid.

Jeremiah was a boy when God called him, and he admitted to God how fearful he was to go and speak God's words. God said, *"I knew you before I formed you in your mother's womb. Before you were born I set you apart and appointed you as my prophet to the nations" (Jeremiah 1:5)*. When you let go and allow God to have his way, then the burden isn't on you to figure everything out.

God cares and is aware of the work you do for him.

One of the coolest Bible heroes who discovered God's calling was Stephen. This guy's job was to take care of widows in the church. He was also great at telling people about Jesus. He did this with so much energy and enthusiasm that the Jewish leaders couldn't argue with him. They became so angry that they stoned him to death! Stephen saw the heavens open up and Jesus himself standing to watch his obedience to the call.

God can use little things he calls us to do to make a *big* difference.

Look at these examples of heroes from the Bible who God called to do simple things...with huge outcomes!

- Daniel—He prayed obediently to God everyday and stood bravely before the entire kingdom for God. God uses Daniel to tell all of the Israelite people that God is with them even though they are being held captive by another nation. Daniel's whole story can also be found in the book of the Bible named after him.
- Nehemiah—A servant to the king, Nehemiah rebuilt the wall of Jerusalem. Nehemiah had many obstacles in his way but kept his attention focused on what he felt God was calling him to do. There were many people who did not want to see Nehemiah succeed in rebuilding the wall. Read the whole book, and see how men tried to trick Nehemiah.
- The boy with the fish and the loaves—In John 6, a boy gives Jesus his own small lunch, and Jesus feeds a huge crowd. It's not about what we bring to Jesus. It's about whether or not we are obedient enough to bring what we have.

63 Who says God isn't funny anyhow?

Gideon was a carpenter with no leadership or battle experience, but God led him and an army to victory with clay pots and lanterns (Judges 6). You have to read this story!

+ EXTRA THOUGHT

A specific word about angels: There would be no need for a book like this if God still used angels as his main mode for telling us our calling. During Old Testament times, there were no copies of God's Word lying in the tabernacle lost and found. So angels and prophets were some of the main ways he communicated specific messages to his people. But who are we to say God won't fall back on the angel option instead of, say, a text? So here is our official stance on hearing your calling from an angel: If an angel tells you to do something, it is God's calling on your life. However, they don't carry angel identification cards from what we can see in the Bible. To identify an angel look for music from out of nowhere, wings, glowing faces, and robes that look the brightest white you've ever seen. From our research, we saw that angels had two main jobs when appearing to mortals: telling people their calling and killing. So if you see an angel and he doesn't say, "Do not be afraid," then be afraid.

64 God helps us knuckleheads by not letting us escape our true calling.

Sometimes we are too hardheaded to catch on to God's plan. He helps us out by pursuing us! That's right, God chases after people. To get one guy's attention, God knocked him out with a bright light and blinded him for days. When we run from our calling, it keeps creeping up everywhere we go. You can't outrun God's plan for your life because he's inescapable.

+ EXTRA THOUGHT

Read the whole story of how the guy who wrote most of the New Testament hunted Christians before he heard his true calling in Acts 9.

YOU KNOW YOU'RE HEARING GOD'S CALL WHEN...

Thoughts 65 to 74

The following thoughts on hearing God's call are guidelines to let you know when you're on the right track...or not so much. The way this works is you have to say, *"You know you're hearing God's call..."* and then read each of the zinger thoughts below.

65
...when your calling is about blessing other people.

Jesus was all about blessing others. You know you are on the right track with your calling when it looks like his. He is our example to follow.

66
...when the things you're doing are bearing the fruit of the Holy Spirit.

Check out Galatians 5:22-23, *"But the Holy Spirit produces this kind of fruit in our lives: love, joy, peace, patience, kindness, goodness, faithfulness, gentleness, and self-control."* When these things are creeping into your life, you know God is at work.

...when it's not all about making you look good in the spotlight.

This can slowly sneak up on you if you're not careful. Your calling may start out right but over time fade into something different than what God originally called you to. Be on guard, and step back every now and then to ask yourself if the calling has become a tool for you instead of you being a tool for God. Basically, don't be a tool, unless you're a tool for God.

...when you are becoming more aware of your own sin.

The closer you grow to God, the more aware you become of how far away you were. God is holy. You only get to have a relationship with God because he sees the holiness of Jesus in us.

...when you are becoming more like Jesus.

You are not alone on this one. Making you like Jesus is actually the job of the Holy Spirit who comes to live inside of you.

...when you are more likely to forgive others for sinning against you.

It's normal for people to struggle with forgiving others. Only the power of God living inside of you can help you take steps toward forgiving others. When you are able to do this, you can know you're hearing and obeying your calling from God.

...when your identity is wrapped more around who Jesus is than who you are.

This doesn't mean you become a zombie for Jesus. John the Baptist said that Jesus must become greater while he became less (John 3:30). Your new starting place becomes Jesus. You will desire to become a great trumpet player (fill in that blank for yourself) so that you can bring glory to him.

...when your calling is about Jesus.

Think about all the good things you see done by people who leave Jesus out of their calling. Don't waste your life. We do good things because of Jesus and for his glory. Don't make the mistake of leaving him out of it.

 ...when you're doing something that makes you uncomfortable.

God uses tough circumstances to mold us. We find out that many times our calling is centered around us becoming more like Jesus. That takes work, and it can be difficult. Proverbs 3:12 says, *"The Lord corrects those he loves, just as a father corrects a child in whom he delights."* If your calling doesn't push you beyond what you think you can do alone, then it might not be from God after all.

You know you're *not* hearing God's call...when your calling hurts other people.

God doesn't like it when people use his name for their own agenda—especially when it hurts people. God won't stand for being used as a club to hit people. If your calling is centered around tearing people down, destruction, ridicule, causing division among believers, or stirring up dissension, *stop it*. Even if your ultimate goal is good, the way you get there is just as important. Find another way.

CHECK YOUR CALLING

Thoughts 75 to 79

How do you know if your call is from God or not? He did tell lots of people crazy things that others didn't understand. From what I can tell, he seems to like keeping it original; so if a burning bush or donkey talks to you, God has already used those bits. Make sure your friends aren't pranking you! Who knows, I could be wrong about God using the donkey thing twice and you may be a modern-day prophet...but just in case, here are some great thoughts on how to dummy-proof your calling.

Your calling should be about bringing more glory to Jesus than to yourself.

This is a simple way to test your calling: If the core idea has more to do with who Jesus is than who you are, then you are on the right track.

If your calling goes against what the Bible says, then it's time to rethink.

If you are not sure if it does, then ask someone who's wise about God's Word to help you dive into Scripture and evaluate it together.

Do wise people think your calling is a good idea? Seek counsel.

This is great advice. Don't go it alone. Ask others who know you well to give input on what you think your calling is.

Don't rush into your calling without some careful planning.

Some things in life need to be done quickly. If it's a no-brainer like saving someone from drowning, then jump in! That's not the time to put a prayer meeting together and leave the person some reading material that could help them learn to swim better. If God is calling you to something big, then you want to do it *right*. So take some time to get advice, and test whether or not this really is God calling you and not the pizza you ate at two in the morning. (That stuff has a way of talking to you, too!)

79

Tell your parents about your calling, and ask their blessing.

God has put your parents in a special role over your life. Even if your parents are not believers in Jesus, they still know you better than you even know yourself. If your parents do not agree with God's calling on your life, it doesn't mean that it's not from God. Stop and do some more thinking, praying, and seeking. Not every calling God gives you is something for you to start right now. God can change your parents' hearts. God will also honor a child that keeps this commandment from Ephesians 6:1: *"Children, obey your parents because you belong to the Lord, for this is the right thing to do."*

HEARING GOD'S CALL IN BETWEEN THE LINES

Thoughts 80 to 83

These thoughts are all about the places and faces we interact with. When we hear God's calling on our lives, it is first going to have an impact on our families and friends we spend our lives with. Even though what God is calling us to is a good thing, we might have conflict with others who don't understand.

80 Hearing God's call usually starts at home...and that can be *hard*.

We all get excited about the mystery of the unknown, but we have to start where we are. The people at home know you best, and that can work for you and against you.

Make your tough decisions now!

Following God's calling is going to be easier in some places than in others. And after you hear God and start making moves to follow your calling, it's going to make some waves. Since you already know this, think ahead about what your new calling is going to call you to change.

Are you going to need to stop some habits or start some new ones? What will you do in the same old situations now that you have a new viewpoint? Nobody makes good decisions when he or she is put on the spot. If you are going to obey God's calling on your life, then he is going to start changing things in and around you. Get yourself ready so when the time comes you won't be caught off guard.

Following God's call will change some friendships.

Sometimes our friends are not our biggest fans. People can be mean. Think about this: The way they treat you may have more to do with how they feel about themselves than how they feel about you. If your calling is from God, then keep on track. Here are some tips on mixing friends with your calling:

- Don't dump everything on your friends in one big public surprise. How would *you* want to be told of a major decision in your friend's life?
- Pray about a time and place to talk with them.
- Give them time to think about it.
- Invite them to join you.
- Trust your friendships to God. Ecclesiastes 3:11 says, *"He has made everything beautiful in its time. He has also set eternity in the hearts of men; yet they cannot fathom what God has done from beginning to end"* (NIV).

The best of us get lost on our way, so put reminders in place to keep your calling top of mind.

Life gets so busy, and hearing God's voice can get lost in the shuffle when we don't have some checks and balances in place to keep us on task. Here are some thoughts to help keep your focus on your calling:

- Write it down where you will read it every day.
- Tell the people you are closest to so they can help keep you on track.
- If there are things you already know will be distractions, then get rid of them *now*.

FINAL THOUGHTS

Thoughts 84 to 99

Nobody ever gets to a place where they hear God's voice perfectly all the time without questioning it. There are distractions in life, and we all have to consistently work on listening purposefully to what God may be saying. Keep these thoughts in mind and keep listening.

84 Accept a challenge.

We can complicate hearing God's call when all we have to do is decide first to do it. There is so much adventure in starting something new and unknown. Go to weamplify.com, and accept a Kingdom Worker Challenge card. Decide before you get there that you will complete whatever it asks you to do. Start your adventure. Get a card.

85 God wants you to find joy in him and the gifts he's given you.

He has gifted you in ways that you perhaps don't even understand yet. When God calls, he will most likely call you to use the very gifts he has hidden within you.

86 Enjoy the journey.

Hearing God's calling on your life and living that out will be the greatest adventure ever. There will be times of joy and times of pain, but hang on tight through it all.

87 Being called by God isn't like what happens in the movies.

No really, it isn't. It's actually better because it's real life.

88 It doesn't all happen overnight.

You know when you want to change and you're excited about your faith and God's calling? It's all going to happen. Sometimes it happens slower than what you want. Relax. Slow down. God's timing is perfect, so don't put a ton of pressure on yourself to get the show on the road. After all, it's God's plan—he will make it work.

Never stop listening because callings change.

The calling you have right now on your sports team may not be the same thing he's calling you to next year. Never stop listening because he's always looking for someone who is willing and available. Attach yourself to him and not the current plan. That way you'll never get separated from what matters most.

 ## Sometimes we don't find success in our calling.

God told Isaiah that his calling was to preach to a people that would never listen to him. Isaiah was still obedient to God's calling even though he knew beforehand that he would not be successful in turning the people back to God. That was not his role. Isaiah found favor in the sight of God for his obedience— that was the true measure of his success.

Don't confuse your calling with God himself.

Even really good things can get in the way of keeping God first. What God calls you to will most likely change over the course of your life; but *he* is unchanging. Hang on to him and not to the work he calls you to do.

Never think you're doing God a favor.

It's true that he loves you and wants you to work in his Kingdom. He is the one who put your gifts within you. But no matter what, with or without your help, God is going to accomplish his will. Remember that you're privileged to work for him and with him.

People who are called to minister professionally (that's their job) aren't better Christians.

No one calling is viewed as more significant than another is to God. We thank God for people who have a ministerial calling because they serve us by helping us grow closer to God.

+ EXTRA THOUGHT

Professional ministry is one of those places where God says, "Follow me...but it won't be easy." James 3:1 says, *"Dear brothers and sisters, not many of you should become teachers in the church, for we who teach will be judged more strictly."*

94 Don't compare callings with other people's.

Comparing callings will always lead to unhappiness. This nasty disease will destroy everything in its path. No matter where you find yourself, there will always be another person who's calling seems better or easier than yours.

95 Don't serve where you are not called!

When you serve where you are not called, you're robbing God and other people, too. You are robbing God because you're not doing what he has planned for you to do, *and* you're robbing another person by doing his or her job. You will always find the most joy when you are working where God intended you to be.

96 Your calling usually starts right where you are.

Right now, it may be best not to start or look for anything new that God is calling you to. Instead, start to see in a new way where you are, who you know, and what you are already doing. How can you do it better and for Jesus so people will know him more?

97

God doesn't call every person to a hut in the Sahara desert.

People have the idea that following God means their life is going to be awful and he will take everything away from them that they've always wanted. The truth is that the good things you want to experience in life actually come from him! He wants to live those moments with you. What future moments do you want to make sure he is a part of in your life?

- Think through the major milestones ahead of you: prom, getting your driver's license, going away to college, your wedding day...
- Invite God now to prepare you for those experiences, and tell him you want him to be the focus of your life.

+ EXTRA THOUGHT

God did call all of the following people to or from a "desert"—a lonely place. God seems to like these lonely places for testing and teaching people—for example, Moses, Abraham, Isaac, Noah, Elisha, Samson, David, Jesus, Elijah, and John the Baptist.

98   Don't be wishy-washy.

Ever know a person who is always changing directions? Even if they are going from one good thing to another, they will never actually do anything. When we ask our Father to tell us what to do and he tells us, we should not doubt him. James 1:5-8 says, *"If you need wisdom, ask our generous God and he will give it to you. He will not rebuke you for asking. But when you ask him, be sure that your faith is in God alone. Do not waver, for a person with divided loyalty is as unsettled as a wave of the sea that is blown and tossed by the wind. Such people should not expect to receive anything from the Lord. Their loyalty is divided between God and the world, and they are unstable in everything they do."*

99   Trust the details of your calling to God.

When God calls you, there are things he takes on as his part and things he gives you to do. So do your part and wait patiently on him to do his. His timing is always better. Remember that he can see how this all ends, so trust him!

CONCLUSION

It is possible to clearly hear God's will for your life. He doesn't want you to be confused and get something so important wrong. Hearing God's voice is a very serious matter that should never be decided upon without lots of prayer. Many people claiming to be working for the Lord have hurt other people. It takes work on our part and practice, but we will hear if we listen and look. Life can be distracting, so be sure to stay focused!